JUPITER

A TRUE BOOK

by

Larry Dane Brimner

Children's Press®
A Division of Grolier Publishing
New York London Hong Kong Sydney
Danbury, Connecticut

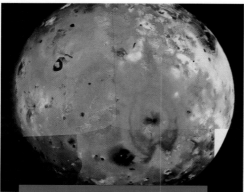

Jupiter's volcanic
moon Io

Subject Consultant
Peter Goodwin
Science Department Chairman
Kent School, Kent, CT

Reading Consultant
Linda Cornwell
Learning Resource Consultant
Indiana Department
of Education

Author's dedication:
For my friends at Naranca
Elementary School
in El Cajon, California.

**Visit Children's Press® on the
Internet at:**
http://publishing.grolier.com

Library of Congress Cataloging-in-Publication Data

Brimner, Larry Dane.
    Jupiter / by Larry Dane Brimner.
       p.   cm. — (A true book)
    Includes bibliographical references and index.
    Summary: Describes the appearance, climate, moons, and exploration
of the largest planet in the solar system.
    ISBN 0-516-21153-6 (lib. bdg.)   0-516-26495-8 (pbk.)
    1. Jupiter—Juvenile literature. [1. Jupiter.] I. Title. II. Series.
QB661.B65 1999
523.45—dc21   98-2951
                                                      CIP
                                                       AC

GROLIER
PUBLISHING

Contents

The Solar System

Venus

Moon

Earth

Asteroid Belt

Saturn

The Giant Planet

Of the nine planets that travel around the Sun, Jupiter stands out as the giant. It is 88,793 miles (143,000 kilometers) across, bigger than any other planet in the solar system. Do you think our Earth is a big place? If Jupiter were a hollow ball, more than 1,300 Earths could fit inside it!

Earth may seem like a big planet, but it is tiny compared to the gigantic size of Jupiter.

Ancient religions believed that Jupiter was the king of all gods.

Early sky watchers named the planets after their gods. They named the giant planet *Jupiter* after the Roman king of the gods and ruler of the sky. This name certainly fits a planet that is bigger than the other eight planets put together.

The Fifth Planet

Jupiter is the fifth planet from the Sun and the nearest "outer planet" to Earth. The "outer planets" are: Jupiter, Saturn, Uranus, Neptune, and Pluto. Except for Pluto, the outer planets are also known as the *Jovian* planets, which means "like Jupiter." These

Jupiter is the fifth planet from the Sun, and it is also the largest.

planets are "gas giants," or made up mostly of whirling gases, just as Jupiter is.

Like the other planets, Jupiter travels around the Sun. It is an average of 483 million miles (780 million km) from the

Sun. Because it is so far away, it takes Jupiter almost 12 Earth-years to make its way around the Sun. It takes Earth just one year—365 days—to orbit the Sun.

As Jupiter orbits the Sun, it also rotates, or spins, on its axis—an imaginary line through the center of the planet. Jupiter spins faster than any other planet. Earth takes 24 hours—one day—to make one rotation. But Jupiter takes just a little less than 10 hours.

Jupiter's Clouds

Jupiter is surrounded by colorful zones, or bands, separated by dark belts. The zones and belts make Jupiter look striped. The zones contain swirls of blue, orange, rust, yellow, light brown, and white. These swirls are storm clouds. They are pushed by

The bands of clouds surrounding
Jupiter make the planet look striped.

Jupiter's clouds come in a variety of colors.

winds that howl along at more than 400 miles (644 km) per hour.

Scientists don't really know why Jupiter's clouds are so colorful. They think it may be because of temperature. The average temperature of Jupiter's clouds is very cold: −186 degrees Fahrenheit (−120 degrees Celsius). Scientists think that when the gases in the clouds freeze, they form crystals that color the clouds.

Jupiter's Great Red Spot

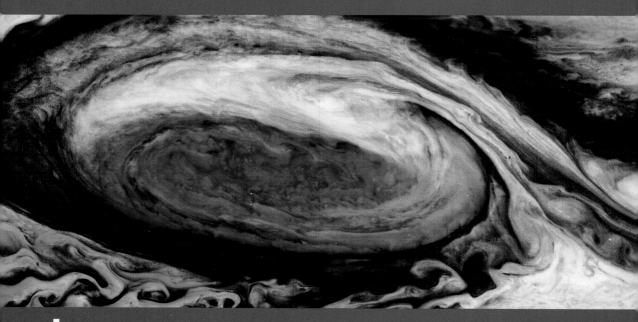

Jupiter's most striking feature is the Great Red Spot. Sky watchers have known about it for more than 300 years. The Great Red Spot is an oval-shaped storm that whirls at a speed of 250 miles (400 km) per hour. This storm is like a hurricane, but much bigger. It is about 15,500 miles (25,000 km) across. That's as wide as two Earths!

The color varies with a cloud's altitude, or how high the cloud is above Jupiter's surface. Jupiter has three layers of clouds. Blue clouds form in the layer closest to the planet's surface. The next layer has brown and white clouds. The clouds at the highest altitude are red.

Jupiter's clouds are so thick that we can't see Jupiter's surface. When we look at Jupiter through a telescope, we see

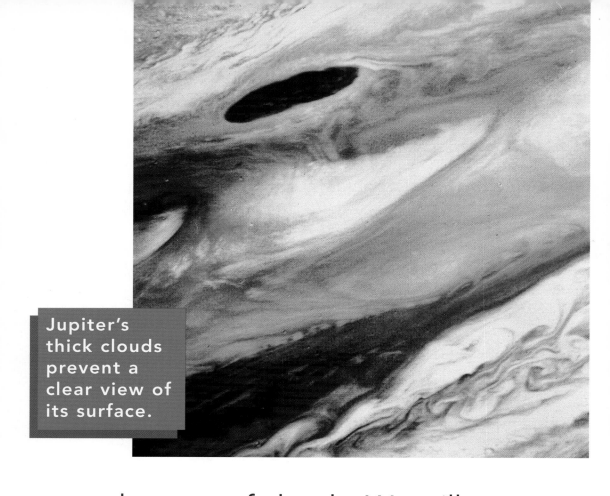

Jupiter's thick clouds prevent a clear view of its surface.

the tops of clouds. We still don't know what is beneath the planet's clouds. But scientists have a good idea of what we might find there.

You would not be able to stand on the surface of Jupiter the way you can stand on Earth's surface. Jupiter's "surface" is not solid. Scientists think it is a liquid. They believe the gases that make up Jupiter's atmosphere change into a liquid deep within the planet's clouds. Scientists also think that deep inside the liquid layer there may be a rocky center, or core.

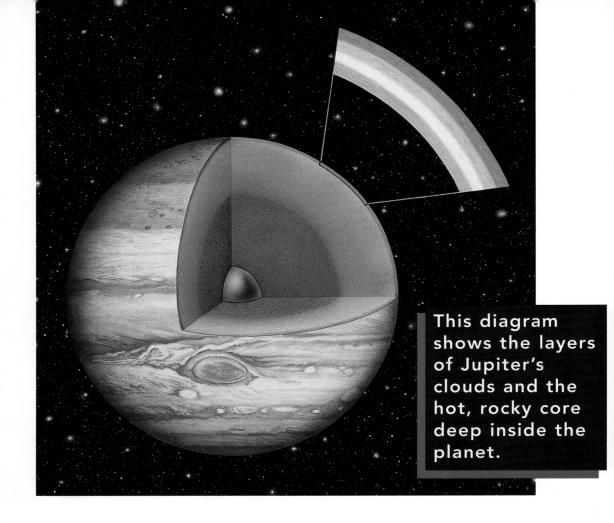

This diagram shows the layers of Jupiter's clouds and the hot, rocky core deep inside the planet.

Jupiter's core may be as hot as 35,500°F (20,000°C). This great heat creates the strong winds that push Jupiter's clouds.

Jupiter's Neighbors

Jupiter has sixteen known moons, and some scientists think there may be more. These moons orbit Jupiter just like our Moon orbits Earth. The four moons nearest Jupiter are small, but the next four are large. These four large moons were discovered

Galileo discovered the four largest moons of Jupiter in 1610.

in 1610 by the Italian astronomer Galileo Galilei (1564–1642) with his homemade telescope. They are named Io, Europa, Ganymede, and Callisto.

Io is one of the most unusual moons in our solar system because it has active volcanoes. These were discovered when

Io is covered with volcanoes.

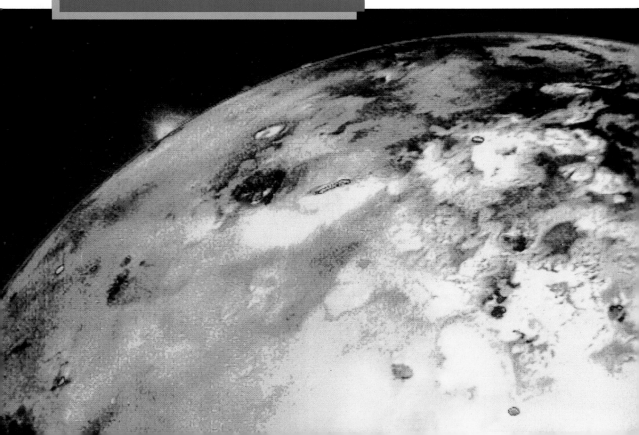

scientists sent probes, or spacecraft, to study and photograph Jupiter and its moons. One probe, *Voyager 1,* pointed its camera at Io and photographed an erupting volcano. Later probes photographed other volcanoes. Before this discovery, scientists thought Earth was the only planet in the solar system with active volcanoes.

Europa is slightly smaller than Earth's Moon. Its surface

Cracks cover Europa's surface.

layer is made of water ice
about 3 miles (5 km) thick.
Photographs show that
Europa seems to be covered

with dark lines. These lines are really cracks where water pushed to the surface and froze. Beneath its icy crust, Europa may have oceans more than 30 miles (50 km) deep.

Jupiter's biggest moon is Ganymede. Ganymede is also the largest moon in the solar system. It's bigger than the planet Mercury! Its surface is covered with rock and ice.

Ganymede is the largest
moon in the solar system.

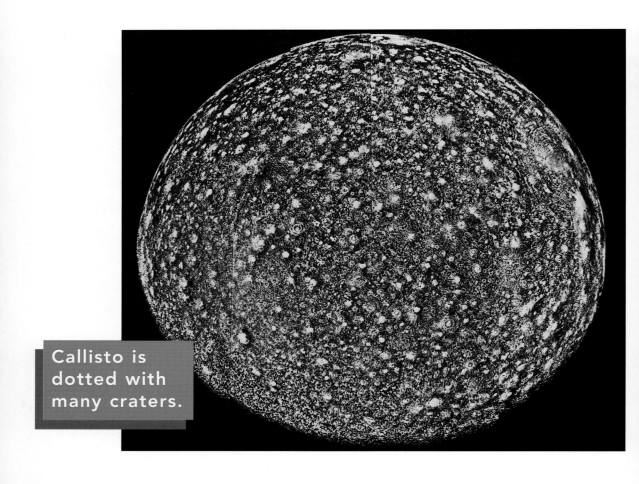

Callisto is
dotted with
many craters.

Callisto is the large moon
farthest from Jupiter. In many
ways, it is like Ganymede. Its
rocky core is surrounded by

ice and more rock. Callisto, however, has more craters, or holes, than any other moon in the solar system. These holes were punched into Callisto's crust by crashing meteorites— large chunks of rock and metal that hit other objects in space.

Jupiter's eight other moons are small and orbit beyond Callisto. Sinope, 15 million miles (24 million km) away, is Jupiter's most distant moon.

Exploring Jupiter

Since the 1970s, probes have explored Jupiter. These spacecraft carry cameras and scientific equipment that tell scientists more about the planet. In 1973, *Pioneer 10* passed within 82,172 miles (132,250 km) of Jupiter's cloud tops and sent more than five hundred photographs back to Earth.

This is one of the earliest photographs of Jupiter, taken by *Pioneer 10*.

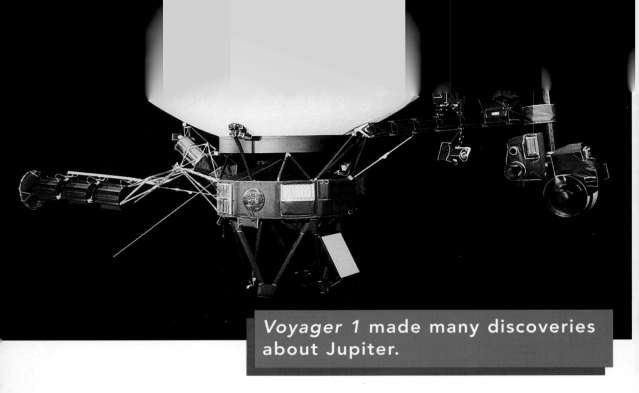
Voyager 1 made many discoveries about Jupiter.

Voyager 1 flew by Jupiter on March 5, 1979. One of its most exciting discoveries was that Jupiter has thin rings around it. Only three other planets in our solar system have rings: Saturn, Neptune, and Uranus.

Rings around the Planet

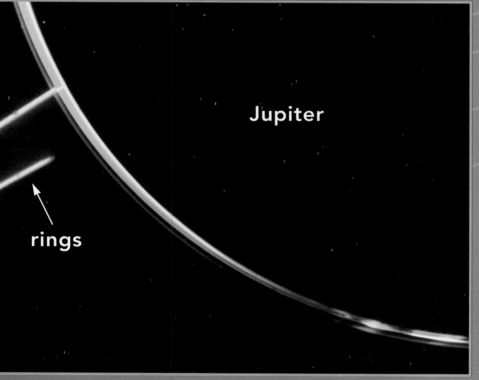

Discovered by *Voyager 1*, Jupiter's rings are thin and not as easily seen as those that surround Saturn. They are made of very small particles of dust and rocky material.

Jupiter

rings

The probe *Galileo* was released into space for its journey to Jupiter.

The *Galileo* spacecraft was launched from Earth in 1989. Six years later, in 1995, it went into orbit around Jupiter for a two-year study of Jupiter's atmosphere and moons.

Galileo's main spacecraft carried a smaller probe that was dropped 120 miles (190 km) into Jupiter's cloudy atmosphere. This smaller probe gave scientists their first real clues as to what

A drawing of *Galileo's* smaller probe as it drops through Jupiter's atmosphere

Jupiter is like beneath its thick cloud tops. The main spacecraft has also given scientists new information about Jupiter's moons.

Impact with a Comet

In 1994, a comet, or giant chunk of ice and dust that orbits the Sun, approached Jupiter. It was named Comet Shoemaker-Levy 9, after the astronomers who first spotted it.

When Shoemaker-Levy 9 passed close to Jupiter,

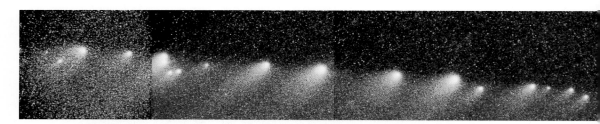

Comet Shoemaker-Levy 9
(top) crashed into Jupiter in
1994. Scientists watched the
comet's impact (bottom).

it broke apart. Between July 16 and 22, 1994, at least twenty large pieces of the comet—some as big as 1.2 miles (2 km) across—crashed into Jupiter. The impacts were so powerful that they sent giant fountains of gas thousands of miles into the atmosphere.

Scientists were able to watch Comet Shoemaker-Levy 9 hit Jupiter. The Hubble Space Telescope, a

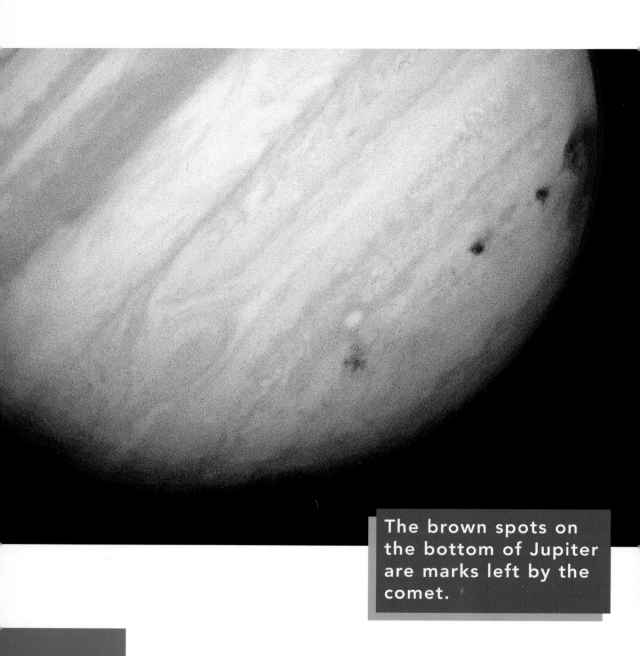

The brown spots on the bottom of Jupiter are marks left by the comet.

telescope orbiting in space, and the *Galileo* spacecraft photographed the event.

Many scientists think Jupiter may be like Earth was when it formed 4.5 billion years ago. By studying Jupiter, we may learn more about how the solar system formed. We may also better understand the early history of our own home planet— Earth.

Jupiter Quick Facts

Diameter	88,793 miles (143,000 km)
Average distance from the Sun	483 million miles (780 million km)
Average cloud temperature	–186°F (–120°C)
Length of day	9 hours 54 minutes
Length of year	11.9 Earth-years
Moons	16 known

Missions to Jupiter

Mission	Launch Date
Pioneer 10 (USA)	March 3, 1972
Pioneer 11 (USA)	April 6, 1973
Voyager 1 (USA)	September 5, 1977
Voyager 2 (USA)	August 20, 1977
Galileo (USA)	October 18, 1989

To Find Out More

Here are more places to learn about Jupiter and other planets in space:

 **Books**

Bailey, Donna. **The Far Planets.** Raintree/Steck-Vaughn, 1991.

Brewer, Duncan. **Jupiter.** Marshall Cavendish, 1993.

Landau, Elaine. **Jupiter.** Franklin Watts, 1991.

Simon, Seymour. **Jupiter.** Morrow & Co., 1985.

Organizations and Online Sites

The Children's Museum of Indianapolis
3000 N. Meridian Street
Indianapolis, IN 46208
(317) 924-5431
http://childrensmuseum. org/sq1.htm

Visit the SpaceQuest Planetarium to see what it has to offer, including a view of this month's night sky.

National Aeronautics and Space Administration (NASA)
http://www.nasa.gov

At NASA's home page, you can access information about its exciting history and present resources and missions.

National Air and Space Museum
Smithsonian Institution
601 Independence Ave. SW
Washington, DC 20560
(202) 357-1300
http://www.nasm.si.edu/

The National Air and Space Museum site gives you up-to-date information about its programs and exhibits.

The Nine Planets
http://seds.lpl.arizona.edu/ nineplanets/nineplanets/

Take a multimedia tour of the solar system and all its planets and moons.

Space Telescope Science Institute
3700 San Martin Drive
Johns Hopkins University
Homewood Campus
Baltimore, MD 21218
(410) 338-4700
http://www.stsci.edu//

The Space Telescope Science Institute operates the Hubble Space Telescope. Visit this site to see pictures of the telescope's outer-space view.

Windows to the Universe
http://windows.engin. umich.edu/

This site lets you click on all nine planets to find information about each one. It also covers many other space subjects, including important historical figures, scientists, and astronauts.

Important Words

altitude how high something is above a planet's surface

astronomer a scientist who studies objects in space

atmosphere the gases that surround a planet

axis an imaginary line about which a planet turns

comet a ball of frozen water, gases, and dust that orbits the Sun

hurricane a storm with very strong winds

Jovian like Jupiter

orbit to travel around an object

probe a spacecraft used to study space

rotate to spin

telescope an instrument that makes far-away objects look closer

volcano a deep crack that spouts hot, liquid rock

Index

Meet the Author

Larry Dane Brimner is the author of more than fifty books for young readers, including these other True Book titles: *E-Mail, The World Wide Web,* and *The Winter Olympics*. A former teacher, he now writes full time and makes his home in San Diego, California.